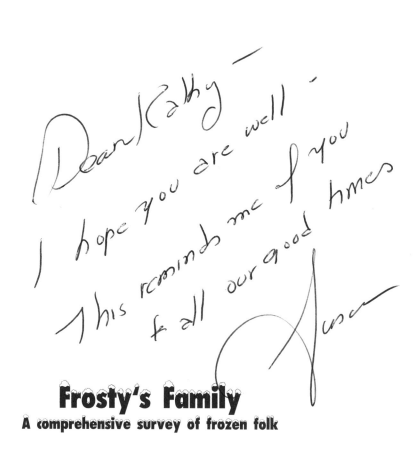

Dear Kathy —

I hope you are well —

This reminds me of you
& all our good times

Susan

Frosty's Family
A comprehensive survey of frozen folk

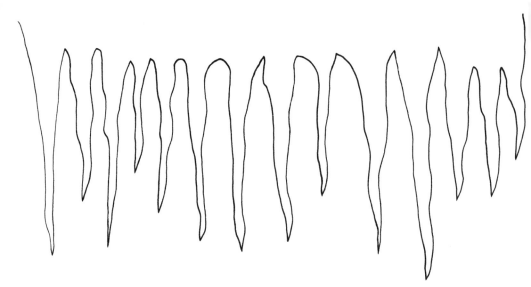

Frosty's Family
A comprehensive survey of frozen folk

Written by David Schecter

Illustrations by Dean Norman

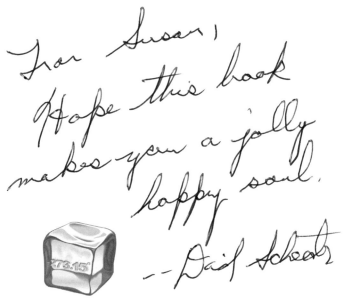

For Susan,
Hope this book
makes you a jolly
happy soul.

-- David Schecter

ABSOLUTE **ZERO** PRESS

Frosty's Family
A comprehensive survey of frozen folk

Published by Absolute Zero Press
P. O. Box 4445
Chatsworth, CA   91313
www.frostysfamily.com

Proudly printed in the United States of America

ISBN: 978-0-9862165-0-3

Layout and design: Teresa Hogenson

Contents

Acknowledgments

Frosty's Family has been drifting around in my head for a long time. It took me decades to complete, because every time I came close to finishing it, another project would take me away from it for a few years. By the time I returned to the book, some of the jokes were either outdated or else just didn't seem as funny as when I first wrote them. This pattern of starting and stopping repeated itself quite a few times as I moved through various careers, until somehow I finally managed to reach the end.

Over the years, many people urged me to keep going, and their positive feedback certainly helped keep the idea alive for me. But special thanks must go to two ladies who had a profound impact on this book: Julie Adams and Barbara Rush. Besides being two of my favorite actresses, both are incredibly intelligent, creative, and well-read. Despite this, they both loved my work-in-progress and their laughter at the snowman gags was exactly what I needed at the time. They both insisted that I finish the book and get it out on the marketplace, but whether they were right or wrong – I leave that up to you, the reader. But I can honestly say that without their enthusiasm, *Frosty's Family* would likely have gone back into my files for another decade or more.

When American Greetings hired me fresh out of college to be a studio (funny) card writer at their Cleveland, Ohio headquarters, I immediately became awestruck by the work of Dean Norman, their top writer/cartoonist. The clarity of his economical drawing style held a special appeal for me, and his art always raised his jokes to the next level. Even his non-studio cards often brought a smile to my face because his art was so beguiling. I want to thank Dean for looking at my original poorly drawn sketches and being able to recognize that they were supposed to be snowmen. He was kind and patient enough to stick with me through all the stops and restarts in this project. I consider myself very fortunate that someone with his talent took my primitive scribblings and made them come alive on the page. I consider myself even luckier to call him a friend.

Finally, much appreciation goes to everyone who decided to buy this book for whatever reason. I hope you get more than a few chuckles out of it.

Preface

I had two goals in writing this book. The first was to shed some much-needed light on a heretofore neglected subject. The second was to sell a few million copies so I wouldn't have to complete any of my other unfinished projects that are in various states of disarray. If I only achieve one of these goals, I truly hope it's the latter.

Introduction

After writing the tune "Frosty the Snowman" in 1950, songwriters Walter "Jack" Rollins and Steve Nelson sent it to singing cowboy Gene Autry, who had released a hit version of "Rudolph the Red-Nosed Reindeer" with the Cass County Boys the year before. Autry recorded their snowman song right away, and from that moment on, Frosty's fame moved inexorably across the nation's pop culture landscape like a smiling, button-nosed glacier.

And just as Rudolph had conquered other media beyond music, so did Frosty. The snowman's reputation spread via a children's book, a three-minute 1954 cartoon, and a 1969 animated TV program narrated by Jimmy Durante. Frosty quickly became everyone's favorite frigid friend, leaving behind other wintry wannabes in his frozen wake. Some of the chilly characters who got wiped off the weather map by Frosty's celebrity status were Jack Frost, Suzy Snowflake, Helen the Hailstone, Blumenthal the Blizzard, and Sylvia Slushpile. Over the years, Frosty's well-known song has been recorded by a wide variety of artists, including The Beach Boys, The Brady Bunch, The Caroleer Singers, Cocteau Twins, Perry Como, The Ray Conniff Singers, The International Childrens' Choir, The Jackson 5, Jan and Dean, Kimberley Locke, Loretta Lynn, Johnny Mathis, The Partridge Family, Bud Roman, and The Ronettes.

In the mid-1950s, writer-director-actor-producer Orson Welles shot a movie based on the untold story of Frosty's later years as a jolly happy soul suffering from back pain and numbness in his extremities. Unfortunately, the studio took the project away from Welles when the picture went way over budget due to the rising cost of artificial snow. The production was reconceptualized as a story about a corrupt police captain in Mexico, with substantial reshoots and re-editing being done.

The movie was eventually released in 1958 under the title *Touch of Evil*. Despite there being absolutely no mention of a snowman or a magical silk hat in the picture, it still has its share of admirers. However, most cinephiles will admit that the film would have been much better if the police captain had smoked a corn cob pipe rather than cigars.

As famous as he is, few facts are known about Frosty. Although his tune claims that he came to life one day, he obviously didn't miraculously appear all by himself. Scientists have proved via laboratory experiments and computer simulations that the spontaneous creation of such a complex being would be mathematically impossible. So, even if Frosty did require a little "magic" to get himself moving, the tunesmiths forgot to tell us where this zero-degree denizen came from in the first place. Nor did the song go into any details about what Frosty's relationship is with others of his snowy ilk. Because even though Frosty is the most illustrious snowman in the world, as anyone who lives in a nippy climate can tell you, he is certainly not the *only* snowman out there.

While much of Frosty's existence remains clouded in mystery, scholars have made substantial progress documenting the history of snowpeople in general. And these discoveries have overwhelmingly disproved what many primitive cultures have believed. One indigenous tribe in the Aleutian Islands actually prays to a mythical snowman that they call "Henai Uta Kaleya," which, roughly translated, means "Frozen Man Who Never Answers Our Prayers." There are also some Siberian Eskimos who believe that a colossal snowman will one day appear and usher in a time of great prosperity, if only because his gigantic carrot nose will feed their entire population for a generation.

Of course, modern science scoffs at such superstitions, instead relying on hard evidence and painstaking studies to draw indisputable conclusions. After decades of study, two environmental researchers from Finland have determined that a colossal snowman could probably only feed those Siberian Eskimos for a few years at best. As for where snowpeople belong on Earth's timeline, their oldest remains date back hundreds of millions of years, give or take hundreds of millions of years. In the winter of 1938, a party of Dutch explorers discovered what was thought to be a very ancient snowman burial ground. Either that or a very modern sheet of ice. Unfortunately, because snowmen don't preserve well, their fossil record is definitely not as complete as it is for other creatures such as boars, ocelots, and pretty much everything else that ever walked, crawled, flew, burrowed, slithered, or swam on this planet.

So how did I, the author, decide to delve into the world of snowpeople? Ever since I was a child, I have been fascinated by creatures made from precipitation. When I was five years old, I had an imaginary friend made entirely out of fog. Unfortunately, it turned out I was merely viewing the world through smudged glasses, and when my mother cleaned my lenses, I lost my best buddy. My most unforgettable encounter with snow occurred the following year, when I fell headfirst off our front porch into an immense snow bank deposited by a recent blizzard. My father heard my muffled screams, ran outside, and grabbed my kicking legs, pulling me to safety. Shortly after that, my parents installed guard rails on the porch and forbade me from ever again doing anything that stupid. There was also a childhood incident when my sister shoved a cherry snow cone down my back, but this isn't the time or place to dredge up such "family issues." On second thought, it might have been *me* who rammed the frozen dessert down *her* back...

Regardless, I've always loved the snow and other forms of solidified water, so it was only natural that I'd eventually decide to work on a project related to wintry weather. After wasting eight years trying to write the world's first *Encyclopedia of Icicles* and finding myself unable to get past the letter "B," I instead decided to turn my attention elsewhere. For inspiration,

I played the song "Frosty the Snowman" almost nonstop for six months, but soon discovered that I couldn't get the damn tune out of my head no matter what else I listened to. Not even The Crazy World of Arthur Brown's "Fire" or Martha and the Vandellas' "Heat Wave" could melt Frosty's musical hold over me. My therapist advised me that the only way I could free myself from this musical madness was to focus on some kind of nonmusical project related to Frosty. Therefore, I decided to write this book about him and his kin. I later discovered that my therapist didn't actually have any kind of degree in counseling or psychology, but was actually a Tupperware salesman. Which at least explained why I was required to purchase three plastic containers at the end of each session.

After many years of research, writing, and editing, the result is the book you're holding in your hands. Unless somebody is holding it for you. Or perhaps it's an e-book you're reading on a video screen? Or maybe all the pages were downloaded wirelessly from some orbiting server into a port implanted in your brain?

Whichever the case, when you read this book you'll quickly realize that it's impossible to stereotype snowmen and snowwomen. While human beings and many other Earthly life-forms follow the normal curve in terms of their characteristics, because snowflakes have six sides, snowpeople have a unique six-arced normal curve, and therefore they exhibit much more variation. For those who wish to delve into this area far beyond the mathematical scope of this book, I recommend meteorologist Vincent Zugbert's landmark article, "A Quantitative Analysis of Gelid Aqueous Beings," published in the November 1982 issue of Cumulonimbus Digest, right below the advertisement for edible barometers.

I sincerely hope that Frosty's Family will change the way people look at snowpeople. Because if it doesn't, that means I probably would have been better off trying to complete my Encyclopedia of Icicles.

This is Frosty the snowman.

This is Frosty's cousin Tommy...

He's a jockey.

This is Frosty's brother-in-law Hadji...

He teaches yoga.

This is Frosty's sister Elsie…

She got a bad haircut.

This is Frosty's aunt Petula...

She needs to reduce her salt intake.

This is Frosty's cousin Leslie...

She had a face-lift.

This is Frosty's uncle Amos...

He's a flasher.

This is Frosty's stepson Morgan...

Smoking stunted his growth.

This is Frosty's uncle Putnam...

He's a boxer.

This is Frosty's wife, Lara...

She's a model.

This is Frosty's brother-in-law Masa...

He's a sumo wrestler.

This is Frosty's niece Prudence...

She lives on the San Andreas Fault.

This is Frosty's aunt Fanny…

She's having an out-of-body experience.

This is Frosty's sister Maisie...

She's been kidnapped.

This is Frosty's cousin Deke…

He's a pool shark.

This is Frosty's cousin Brett…

He lives in a penthouse.

This is Frosty's nephew Peter…

He's a chim'ney sweep.

This is Frosty's aunt Julie...

She's a nonconformist.

This is Frosty's great-grandfather Walter…

He's discovered the secret of eternal life.

This is Frosty's aunt Coleen…

She's traveling down Memory Lane.

This is Frosty's uncle Otto...

He likes beer.

This is Frosty's uncle Penrod…

He's feeling passé.

This is Frosty's aunt Lorene…

She's in traction.

This is Frosty's brother Nick...

He's a contortionist.

This is Frosty's cousin Lizabeth...

She's a spy.

This is Frosty's brother Lionel…

He's taking the day off.

This is Frosty's nephew Tab...

He's breakdancing.

This is Frosty's granddaughter Connie...

She's diving for pearls.

This is Frosty's son Mac...

He works out.

This is Frosty's son Robert...

He's having a moment of self-awareness.

These are Frosty's great-aunts
Marigold and Priscilla…

They're staying warm.

This is Frosty's uncle Willard…

He's in a police line-up.

This is Frosty's nephew Kyle...

He has the wanderlust.

This is Frosty's aunt Penelope...

She can't remember where
she left her hat.

This is Frosty's brother Joey…

He's too literal.

This is Frosty's uncle Mario…

He's studying his genealogy.

This is Frosty's son-in-law Duncan...

He's made of frozen Scotch.

This is Frosty's great-grandson Blake...

He's a lifeguard.

This is Frosty's nephew Ingram...

He's got dandruff.

This is Frosty's son Luthor...

He's a dock worker.

This is Frosty's niece Shaina…

She's body-surfing.

This is Frosty's nephew Sasha...

He's made of heavy water.

This is Frosty's cousin Kenny...

He hates living in a dog park.

This is Frosty's niece Eunice…

She's camouflaged.

This is Frosty's nephew Fenton...

He's looking for his contact lens.

This is Frosty's sister-in-law Sheba...

She's shy.

This is Frosty's grandson Timmy...

He can dunk.

This is Frosty's cousin Travis...

He has a slipped disc.

This is Frosty's aunt Zola...

She's paranoid.

This is Frosty's sister Lenora...

She just returned from a trip to Acapulco.

This is Frosty's niece Helga...

She's doing her morning sit-ups.

This is Frosty's daughter Imogene...

She's playing hopscotch.

These are Frosty's cousins Ray, Fay, and Kay...

They're on an escalator.

This is Frosty's aunt Gene...

She has agoraphobia.

This is Franz...

He's Frosty's evil twin.

This is Frosty's daughter Edith...

She's walking her pet.

This is Frosty's distant uncle Josh...

He lived back in Jurassic times.

This is Frosty's uncle Ollie...

He escaped from jail.

These are Frosty's cousins Nan and Jan...

They're conserving water.

This is Frosty's daughter Francine...

She wins wet T-shirt contests.

This is Frosty's grandson Bucky…

He's detail oriented.

This is Frosty's cousin Duke…

He's a rodeo star.

This is Frosty's great-grandmother Anita...

She's farsighted.

This is Frosty's daughter Allene...

She had a nose job.

This is Frosty's brother-in-law Ulrich...

He's trying to touch his toes.

This is Frosty's cousin Lupe...

She's winking at a cute guy.

This is Frosty's great-uncle Jacques...

It's his first day at a nudist colony.

This is Frosty's son-in-law Errol…

He's a pirate.

This is Frosty's mother, Fritzi...

She's got termites.

This is Frosty's cousin Beasley...

He fainted.

This is Frosty's aunt Velma...

She's gargling.

These are Frosty's step-cousins…

They live in an apartment building.

This is Frosty's granddaughter Naomi…

She spent too long in the sauna.

This is Frosty's great-great-great-great-great-great-great-great-great-grandson Zebulon...

He traveled back in time
from the 23rd Century.

This is Frosty's uncle Seth...

He's Egyptian.

This is Frosty's brother Harry…

He entertains at children's parties.

This is Frosty's cousin Xavier…

He's stuck in quicksnow.

This is Mimsy...

Frosty's half-sister.

This is Frosty's sister-in-law Audrey…

She's on a cruise.

This is Frosty's cousin Lars...

He's been reincarnated.

This is Frosty's sister Matilda…

She uses water softener.

This is Frosty's nephew Ed…

He's a hockey goalie.

This is Frosty's sister Estelle...

She hates to exercise.

This is Frosty's uncle Andre…

He was unable to avoid foreclosure.

This is Frosty's daughter-in-law Valerie…

She works at a theme park.

This is Frosty's daughter Joyce…

She's a pole dancer.

This is Frosty's uncle Rex…

He survived death row.

This is Frosty's daughter Cleo…

She's keeping a low profile.

These are Frosty's grandsons
Doug and Tug...

They're playing leap-frog.

This is Frosty's son Ty..

He's into body-piercing.

This is Frosty's aunt Avalon…

She's a fortune teller.

This is Frosty's cousin Syd...

He has an inner-ear disorder.

This is Frosty's sister Nessie…

She's letting off some steam.

This is Frosty's daughter Danielle…

She just got a massage.

This is Frosty's granddaughter Deirdre...

She likes heavy metal.

This is Frosty's aunt Portia...

She has cellulite.

This is Frosty's great-granddaughter
June...

She can't wait to reach puberty.

This is Frosty's cousin Norton...

He's assumed the fetal position.

This is Frosty's brother Elbert...

He tried to prevent the construction
of a new road.

This is Frosty's cousin Cyril...

He's an Elvis impersonator.

This is Frosty's daughter Lorna…

She's an escape artist.

This is Frosty's great-granddaughter Patsy…

She's somersaulting.

This is Frosty's mother-in-law Wilma…

She's making a ritual sacrifice.

This is Frosty's uncle Mitch...

He's a politician.

This is Frosty's brother Basil…

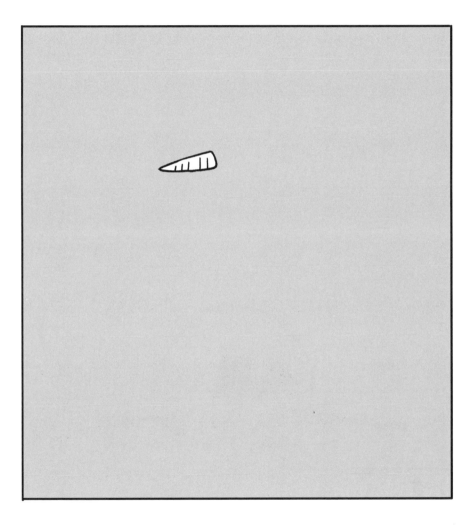

He lives in London.

This is Frosty's great-grandson Graydon…

He's sneaking up.

This is Frosty's son Gilbert...

He's into extreme sports.

This is Frosty's daughter Barbara…

She's on-line.

This is Frosty's sister Deanna…

She was catching some rays.

This is Frosty's granddaughter Simone...

She lost a karate fight.

This is Frosty's sister Sonya...

She's a ballerina.

This is Frosty's brother Farley...

He drives a monster truck.

This is Frosty's uncle Xeno…

He's from Greece.

This is Frosty's niece Fawn…

She's a cheerleader.

This is Frosty's uncle Murdock...

His relatives are coming for a visit.

This is Frosty's cousin Gerry…

He's a survivalist.

This is Frosty's sister Beulah…

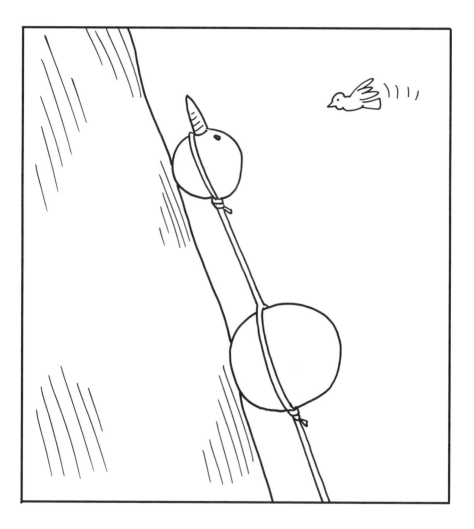

She's climbing Mt. Everest.

This is Frosty's aunt Olivia…

She's delusional.

This is Frosty's brother Nestor…

He's a hybrid.

This was Frosty's uncle Abner…

He's an arson victim.

This is Frosty's great-grandfather Itzy…

He uses a walker.

This is Frosty's brother Tony…

He's nosy.

These are Frosty's cousins
Mona and Leopold…

They're Salsa dancing.

This is Frosty's sister-in-law Linda...

She's got chapped lips.

This is Frosty's brother Jacob…

He lives on a floodplain.

This is Frosty's granddaughter Ruthie...

She shouldn't have used a hair dryer.

This is Frosty's cousin Dori...

She's seeing a shrink.

This is Frosty's brother-in-law Omar...

He's afraid of heights.

This is Frosty's sister Christy...

She runs a day care center.

This is Frosty's great-uncle Rufus...

He lives near a nuclear power plant.

This is Frosty's aunt Greta...

She's trying to improve her circulation.

This is Frosty's grandmother Selma...

She's taking a siesta.

This is Frosty's niece Octavia...

She bungi-jumped.

This is Frosty's cousin Dobie...

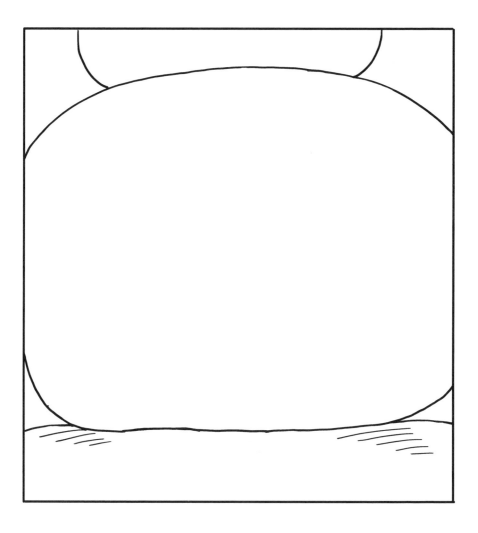

He's on steroids.

This is Frosty's cousin Winnie...

She's made of acid snow.

This is Frosty's brother-in-law Spence...

He's doing push-ups.

This is Frosty's father, Freddie...

He's a workaholic.

This is Frosty's great-grandmother Dorothy...

She wants to move to the countryside.

This is Frosty's father-in-law Jocko...

He's sucking in his gut to impress
some babes.

This is Frosty's sister-in-law Gloria...

She's saying her prayers.

This is Frosty's grandfather Hollis...

He's about to meet his Maker.

This is Frosty's cousin Brad…

He's hiding from the police.

This is Frosty's nephew Alexander...

His doctor has him drinking
plenty of fluids.

This is Frosty's aunt Ramona...

She should have taken the ski lift.

This is Frosty's son-in-law Cool Water...

He's listening for buffalo.

This is Frosty's niece Millie…

She's involved in a whiplash suit.

This is Frosty's cousin Dwight…

He was created by Dr. Frankenstein.

This is Frosty's aunt Jennifer…

She hates her family.

This is Frosty's uncle Russell…

He's the victim of identity theft.

This is Frosty's great-aunt Katy…

She left her brain to science.

This is Frosty's uncle Jon…

He's sweating.

This is Frosty's cousin Boris…

He's in the Witness Protection Program.

This is Frosty's nephew Porter...

He belongs to Mensa.

This is Frosty's brother Sven...

He's helping his son watch the parade.

This is Frosty's sister Karen…

She's modular.

This is Frosty's cousin Monika...

She's considering cosmetic surgery.

This is Frosty's son Nate...

He's multitasking.

This is Frosty's son Jason…

He's a lookout.

These are Frosty's cousins Del, Mel, Belle, Adele, Nell, and Joelle...

They're playing rugby.

This is Frosty's daughter Frostea...

She likes to eat spicy food.

This is Frosty's uncle Warren...

He rides horses.

This is Frosty's uncle Scott…

He has love handles.

This is Frosty's grandmother Aurora…

She's contemplating the meaning of life.

This is Frosty's son Louie…

He joined the circus.

This is Frosty's grandson Payson…

He's studying evolution.

This is Frosty's niece Rose...

She wears hair extensions.

This is Frosty's nephew George…

He's a super-hero.

This is Frosty's aunt Tess...

She suffers from migraines.

These were Frosty's brother Kelso and his sister-in-law Modesty…

They were a celebrity couple.

This is Frosty's cousin Mollie…

She's antisocial.

This is Frosty's cousin Holly...

She works in the frozen food business.

This is Frosty's sister Marcella...

She's in search of distant relatives.

This is Frosty's grandson Lloyd...

He's backpacking.

This is Frosty's aunt Adelaide…

She's having hot flashes.

This is Frosty's sister Bertha...

She's a bodybuilder.

This is Frosty's grandfather Zachary...

He's enjoying his rocking chair.

This is Frosty's daughter Piper...

She needs her space.

This is Frosty's great-aunt Jeanne...

She has separation anxiety.

This is Frosty's brother Irving…

He's made of carbonated water.

This is Frosty's sister Suzanne...

She's depressed.

This is Frosty's brother-in-law Charlton…

He's been retrofitted for earthquakes.

This is Frosty's daughter Una...

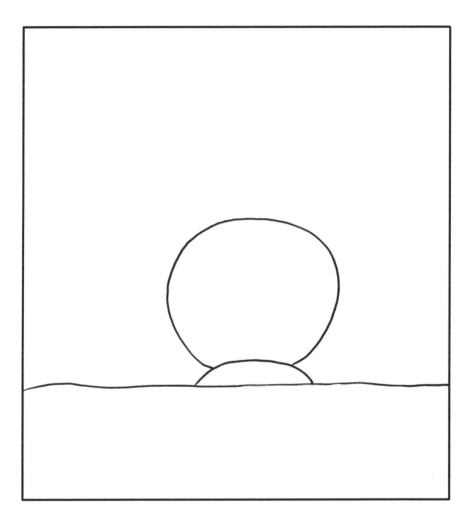

She's a spelunker.

This is Frosty's son Randy…

He's a defensive lineman.

This is Frosty's uncle Wyatt...

He's an air traffic controller.

This is Frosty's son Dirk…

He's in the lotus position.

This is Frosty's daughter-in-law Cinda...

She has multiple personalities.

This is Frosty's cousin Sam...

He's obsessive-compulsive.

This is Frosty's brother Herman...

He's fasting to protest global warming.

Epilogue

Whether going by the name "Global Warming," "The Greenhouse Effect," "Climate Change," or "It's Too #$@&!*% Hot For December," *Homo sapiens'* impact upon Earth's weather patterns might end up being as disastrous to snowpeople as that asteroid was to the dinosaurs. One only hopes that politicians can get their act together to figure out how to minimize the damage as much as possible, and that everyone will eventually realize that the same brains who figured out how to make computers, spaceships, the Internet, and spray-on hair also have a pretty good idea of what's been happening to our climate. Or before long, the only way you might be able to view an actual snowman will be in a freezer at your local zoo.

About the Authors

David Schecter began his writing career working for greeting card, licensing, and toy companies, Sunday magazines, and pretty much anyone else who could cut a paycheck that wouldn't bounce. He studied film and screenwriting at USC and UCLA, and is still waiting to hear back from some of the producers he sent his scripts to over 25 years ago. In 1996, Schecter co-founded the acclaimed Monstrous Movie Music soundtrack CD label, which has contributed music to motion pictures, television shows, and commercials. He is considered the world authority on classic science fiction and horror film music, due to the fact that nobody else wanted that distinction. He also helped create Your Imagination Presents, an audio label designed to teach young children creative and visual thinking via a new form of musical storytelling. Schecter represents the estates of film composers and music publishers, and he also owns a film music publishing company. In his spare time, he can often be found helping computer-illiterate friends deal with problems they created when they clicked on an "install" button when they shouldn't have. He is the proud owner of two Scottish Terriers who don't pay attention to anything he says except *"Supper time!"*

Dean Norman has had a long career writing and drawing for many projects, including television, magazines, newspapers, comics, and children's books. Some of the characters he's worked on include The Archies, Bugs Bunny, Daffy Duck, Doctor Dolittle, Elmer Fudd, The Pink Panther, Porky Pig, Roland and Rattfink, Sabrina the Teenage Witch, Tijuana Toads, Tom and Jerry, and Tweety and Sylvester. He was employed by both American Greetings Corporation and Hallmark, and is one of the finest greeting card writer/illustrators in history. Norman claims to have had vast experience making snowmen, snow balls, and snow forts, all of which melted long ago, so we'll just have to take his word on that. Now semi-retired, he spends much of his time walking the dogs, paddling a canoe, and playing table tennis.

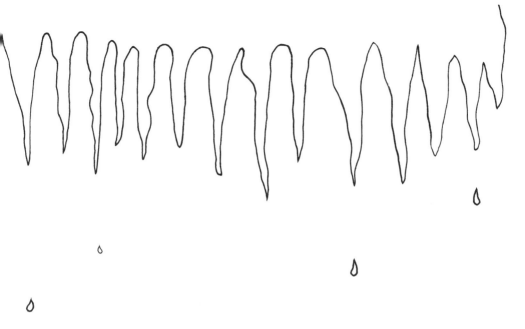